In Pursuit of Me
Guided Journal

Amber Zealous

IN PURSUIT OF ME GUIDED JOURNAL

Please direct all copyright inquiries to:

B.O.Y. Publications, Inc.
c/o Author Copyrights
P.O. Box 262
Lowell, NC 28098
betonyourselfent.com

ISBN: 978-1-955605-83-0

Cover and Interior Design: B.O.Y. Enterprises, Inc.

Printed in the United States.

Dear Reader,

As a woman, I have experienced several situations in my life that made me question who I am. I desired to be seen, chosen, and significant in my own way. As I journeyed, there were many situations that caused me to lose sight of who I was, or thought I was. I wrestled with shame, doubt, fear, toxic thinking and behaviors. I found myself conforming to what others thought I should be in hopes of being accepted and validated. I spent what seemed like endless days feeling strange, because I was trying to be what others said I should be instead of embracing who I was... the authentic me...the flawed yet very much still beautiful version of me.

People love to tell you what you need to do, how you should behave and how you should react, but no one speaks on the importance of understanding and addressing the cycles that keep us stagnant, lost, or on self-destructive paths. As far as I can remember, my life seemed to be very different from others around me. Growing up in a functional dysfunctional family has a way of creating a surreal reality or impractical delusion. I know that my parents' efforts were grounded in love but many times it was also entangled with trauma. So, I made the best choice when it came to viewing the reality. Yes you guessed it, I chose delusion!!! I spent hours alone in my room, playing with Barbie dolls, and acting out all my dreams for the future. Yet, I still believed that being a wealthy stay at home wife with no kids was completely possible. I had no idea that by the time I was eleven my family would experience my sister having a life-changing medical event.

This was when I first started over developing the strengths that would eventually become weaknesses. I learned to be resilient, find a way out of no way, push through, and keep going. The thing is everyone loves to share that the "WAR" was won, but they hardly ever talk about the loss that came with the win. The experiences that I encountered, I made it through them, but I lost sense of who I was in each one.

By age eleven, I learned how to navigate parents being away so much due to taking care of my sister, but I lost a sense of security. By 13, I learned how to avoid my mom giving me the silent treatment, but I lost a sense of autonomy and individuality. When I was raped at 15, I learned how to seek help, and speak up for myself, but also I lost my confidence and transparency, silenced my voice, diminished my self-worth, and changed the entire trajectory of relationships with the opposite sex. When I became a mother at 18, I learned how to navigate motherhood, but I lost my youth. When I decided to be a live-in girlfriend at 19, I learned how to manage a household and have a relationship, but I lost the opportunity to build and discover myself.

When I was 22, I learned that when people treat you poorly it is important to set boundaries and space when needed. Yet, when my mom died unexpectedly, we were not on the best terms due to me setting a boundary. After her death, I lost my courage to set boundaries, speak candidly, and walk away because, what if? What if I stop talking to this person and they die like my mom did? As I said, boundaries went out the window.

Life was heavy trying to navigate that complicated grief. Had I not been so stubborn that day, maybe our last conversation could have been meaningful. I could have told her that I love her. Life found me full of grief every birthday. I made it hard for others to celebrate me on Mother's Day because my heart was just heavy. I carried that with me daily, yet I pushed through. By that time, I was a mother of 4 who couldn't handle celebrating being a mother because of the weight of grief.

After a while, life seemed to even out. At least, that's what I thought, but yea.... not so much. My Dad died when I was 27. Sigh, there I was in this world trying to establish roots for my own lil family and my own roots were snatched up unexpectedly. When my father took his last breath, I lost clarity, support, and a sense of connection. I felt so alone although I was surrounded by many. No mom, no dad ... say what? I lost my desire to thrive. I no longer desired marriage because I was resentful and I shifted blame on him that had he not waited so long, my parents would have been able to see me get married. His delay and their deaths meant I wouldn't be able to have the wedding I planned when I was 7.

By the age of 30, I learned motherhood was about doing better than the day before, and to celebrate the small victories. I understood that no matter how much life, love, sex, and children you give a man, if that man doesn't see your value, you will still have to track him down at 4am about 2-3 times a month. I had a better concept of how credit worked, and I learned how to change locations with ease since I moved about every year. But by this age what was losses, now were gains. I gained massive responsibility, limited support, disappointment, heartache, complacency, the inability to be transparent or ask for help, self-hate, loneliness, and resentment. Everything about life was mundane. I was worried about everything from finances, to kids, to relationships, to work. I mean everything. Then, I got laid off and I decided to go back to school. I stopped checking that man's phone. I noticed my heartache seemed a bit less heavy concerning the loss of my parents, and my kids were not bad. They were actually pretty awesome. I had friends, and hadn't had to get a payday loan in a minute. Life seemed to even out. I got a great job. I had another set of twins, finished school, purchased a house, and life didn't seem as heavy.

By 32, I had 6 kids with one man with whom I invested 14 years, and even with all those years we were somehow still at square one. I was not happy but I also wasn't leaving because like my daddy always said, "No man wants a ready made family," so I believed this was what we would refer to as ride or die. The way I died so many times, I'm sure I was a cat in another life. I won't say that he didn't love me or that he was a bad man. What I will say is he loved me the best way he knew how. I remember saying to God, this is not anything like I imagined so I'm just assuming my purpose in life is to be a mother. Everything kicked into high gear, and I became fueled by my six.

I made out a plan for what I wanted their lives to look like compared to what my life was. My entire mission was to create an atmosphere for them to be whoever they wanted to be. I desired a better neighborhood, resources for sports, travel, appearances, and the opportunity to see that even when all the odds seem to stacked up against you can still WIN. Just because your win doesn't look like someone else's doesn't make it any less of a win. I invested 7 years of hard work, dedication, devotion, harvesting, and pouring into my children not even realizing that I had no clue who I was.

I started to form my identity in their achievements. I created my identities based on my relationships. I learned how to show and hide versions of myself because, who am I? I kept trying to hide the pieces of me that were affected by the losses and gains. Yet, this worked for an extremely long time until my daughter was murdered at the age of 19.

I remember thinking, "This can't be life." But it surely it was, a loss of this magnitude, unexpectedly and complicated. The overwhelming sense of failure, confusion, and sheer heartbreak shattered me completely. It's one thing losing parents and losing a sense of your past. It's an entirely different beast having to bury your future. Nothing made sense. I checked out mentally, spiritually, and a few times physically. I remember thinking, "My God, what have I done that my life has been hard, so heavy, so very difficult?" I asked but heard nothing back. The immense amount of anger towards God was sure to get me promoted to hell. Yet again I pushed through. But this time, I gained a new "I'm fine" personality. The hours became days, days became weeks, weeks turned into months, and the hurt seemed to get worse each day. I blamed myself for not being God and somehow preventing what had taken place. Crazy I know, remember I told you I chose delusion many years ago, it's not always easy to put that down. God began to speak to me and remind me that He is a strategic God. He placed people, places, and so much more to help me navigate the seasons. What I thought was hard, were actually seasons of stretch, preparation, and provision. I was able to see how things were always working together for my good.

At age 11, I had a nephew and cousins that, even when I didn't want to be left alone, they made sure to do the opposite. (I wasn't alone.) When I was 13 , my 1st friendship established on the foundation of "You not dressing out for gym? … Me either." She had full autonomy and didn't mind being who she was. (Strategic Connections) When I was 15, a set of 4 girls I met at the rape crisis center, sadly understood what I was feeling, and every Tuesday and Thursday we got to say all the things aloud that we were forced to say quietly. (Support & Inclusiveness)

At 19, my oldest sister, a hidden treasure and wealth of knowledge showed me what my mother never showed, which was transparency, rawness, honesty, and grace. Every day we spent in her room, kitchen, and deck helped to mold me into a better mother, woman, and overall person. Being able to see the humanity in my hero allowed me to grasp the concept that she was my sister, but also see that she was a mother, a woman that made poor choices, and that had her experiences with love and life.

Each stage of my life, God was there strategically placing people and things to push me through to show me aspects of what the things that I may have lost should look like. No matter if it was grace, strength, style, confidence, or whatever it was, God orchestrated ways to pour it back into me. So many years He planted many seeds in me, some bared fruit, many laid dormant, but all rooted in finding me. It has been the journey to find me that I encountered God in many ways. My hope is that this guided book helps readers to see that imperfection, failures, and disappointment, all fine tune your faith. There are going to be times that you are not the best version of yourself, your finances are in shambles, and your kids go left when you clearly said go right. There will be times that no one may actually see you, or that everyone can see you. No matter how the days or years may leave you broken or together, see power in the pieces. Sometimes its when we are lost in the pieces that we can pursue ourselves the most.

In spite of the things that you have experienced, there is purpose in your pain. I don't look like what I've been through. I did not perish. Agony didn't harden my heart, and even with all my experiences, failures, imperfections, and delusion, I thank God that my life will be a reminder that God is good. May every entry and shared experience in the book of me unpacking emotions, trauma, and heartache out loud speak and heal places that so many of us try to hide or silence. As you embark on this journey, In Pursuit OF ME – May your pursuit of you be intensified and may your encounters with God be magnified.

Best Regards,
Amber Zealous

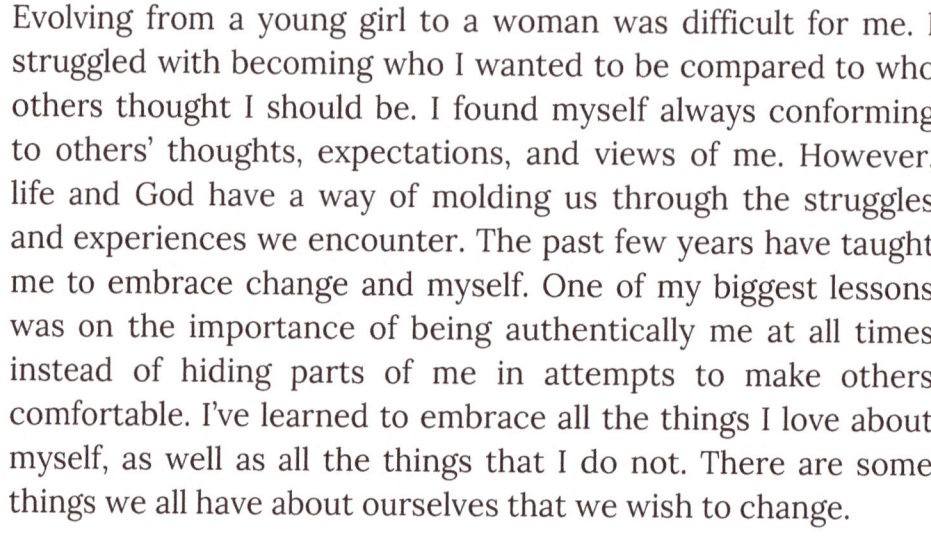

DAY 1

Evolving from a young girl to a woman was difficult for me. I struggled with becoming who I wanted to be compared to who others thought I should be. I found myself always conforming to others' thoughts, expectations, and views of me. However, life and God have a way of molding us through the struggles and experiences we encounter. The past few years have taught me to embrace change and myself. One of my biggest lessons was on the importance of being authentically me at all times instead of hiding parts of me in attempts to make others comfortable. I've learned to embrace all the things I love about myself, as well as all the things that I do not. There are some things we all have about ourselves that we wish to change.

Today, embrace all the things that you love about you, discover all the things that you do not. Change what you can and embrace the things that you can not. Understand what seems like brokenness is actually all the pieces of you that fit together perfectly for who God ordained you to be.

"She is clothed with strength and dignity, and she laughs without fear of the future." **-Proverbs 31:25**

Today's Reflection

M T W Th F S Su   Date: _____

Describe who you are. What do you love most about yourself?
What do you wish to change & why?

_____

_____

_____

_____

_____

_____

_____

_____

_____

_____

_____

_____

_____

_____

_____

_____

_____

_____

_____

_____

_____

_____

DAY 2

One of the things that I always had was a strong imagination. If it were a fantasy or dream world that could be created, I definitely did that! I listened to so many people say how delusional I was in my thoughts and actions as a child, that as I grew into adulthood, I kept my thoughts sheltered in fear of what others might think. I thought small because that made more sense to others than thinking big. When the truth is that I always had the vision, but it wasn't that the vision was unrealistic. It was the lack of execution and planning that was tied to the vision. Without vision, you are navigating the world blindly. When you operate without vision and outside of alignment with God, you experience continuous seasons of missed opportunities, stumbling, and stagnancy. It is imperative that you have vision, but also have a plan. As you shift from just thinking to action, there will be people, places, and things that will no longer align with your vision. In this season, I pray that God allows you to see yourself how He sees you. That way you can see yourself right, other people right, and your seasons right. As you ponder on what the vision is, ask God to reveal the plan and how you can determine the steps to achieve it.

The distance between expectation and execution is prayer, consistency, planning, & effort.

"If people can't see what God is doing, they stumble all over themselves; But when they attend to what he reveals, they are most blessed." **-Proverbs 29:18**

Today's Reflection

M T W Th F S Su   Date: _____

**What is the biggest vision you have for your life? What do you
need to achieve the vision?**

_____

_____

_____

_____

_____

_____

_____

_____

_____

_____

_____

_____

_____

_____

_____

_____

_____

_____

_____

_____

DAY 3

One of the few things that has kept me stagnant in all areas of my life has been self-doubt and fear. When I think back to when I was in the midst of evolving into a woman, I can recognize themes and situations that caused me to internalize defective thought processes of what was deemed right and wrong as well as what was within reach. I was always worried about what others would think or say. What I learned is that people will have something to say no matter if you are doing nothing or something.

One thing we don't always take into account is that many of our core beliefs are given to us by our parents. Not always intentional, but very impactful. When I think about it, I was conditioned to settle for less because more was just not possible. Just work, keep your head above water, and take care of what needs to be taken care of. When the truth is that whatever you truly desire is attainable, and it's located on the other side of self-doubt and fear. God is able to do exceedingly abundantly above all that we ask or think, according to the power. So why are we just settling for the bare minimum????

Your purpose and power don't need the approval of man, and it is not always determined by overplanning either. I once heard faith defined as still believing with your heart, mind, and spirit despite what you see with your eyes. Maybe the reason you are doubting yourself is because you are doubting God. We cannot be in true alignment with God if we have a poor self-image. God created you to be like no other. There is not one single person on this earth who is identical in all aspects. That something different is the clue to what God is calling you to do. We can not be afraid to be who God has called us to be. When we are operating in fear, we become double-minded and easy to trap by the enemy. Those "What If" scenarios that we replay in our minds keeps us stagnant. Nowhere in God's promise in our lives will you find self-doubt and fear. God is waiting on you. To fully understand who God has called you to be also means understanding who God is and how you have been created in His image with purpose. Embracing that overwhelming feeling of who you desire to be could be the key to unlocking your greater purpose and the purpose of the people connected to you.

"For God has not given us a spirit of fear, but of power and of love and of a sound mind." **2 Timothy 1:7**

Today's Reflection

M T W Th F S Su   Date: _____

How is self doubt and fear holding you back? Who do you desire to be?

_____
_____
_____
_____
_____
_____
_____
_____
_____
_____
_____
_____
_____
_____
_____
_____
_____
_____
_____
_____
_____
_____
_____
_____
_____

DAY 4

There was a time in my life when I was unsure who I was, and consistently found myself conforming to fit it. I was attempting to live by what I was taught as a child, while also adjusting to what I learned on my own through interacting with others. Values or what some may call a moral compass is a direct correlation to how you lead in your day-to-day world and determines if you are building purposeful connections or closing doors of opportunity. Values are the core of who we are. The foundation to our values are typically fostered as children by our parents, siblings, teachers, childhood friends, and spiritual leaders. When you think of the word leader, do you see yourself? Or does someone else come to mind first?

Learning to lead BOLDLY was a challenge for me. That's because I was conditioned to be submissive and silent; that being bold, confident, and speaking up for yourself was being rebellious, and having friends or desiring to experience life outside of family would lead to destruction. When the truth is, those things are just like everything else, they require a healthy balance. When you look through the stories of the Bible, God used people that were different, that were not perfect and gave them purpose. We are supposed to be able to listen to the experience and wisdom of others but never replace their perspective over God. The word says in 1 Corinthians 15:33 that "Bad company corrupts good character" which means we have to be mindful of the cups we drink from when it comes to thoughts, values, and actions. It was not until I encountered God personally that I began to lead boldly and intentionally in my life. This is when I understood that the reason that I always struggled to FIT IN, was because God had already destined me to STAND OUT. Leading is not about a title or not always specific assignment but is a level of self-awareness of

- Who you are
- What you believe & why you believe it
- Embracing your God given gifts & purpose
- Understanding and maintaining boundaries
- Being unashamed to shift from expectations to execution.

Are you leading or are you lingering?

"For I can do everything through Christ, who gives me strength."

-Philippians 4:13

Today's Reflection

M   T   W   Th   F   S   Su   Date: _____

Are you leading in actions?
Do you allow your values to vary by company? If so, why?

_____

_____

_____

_____

_____

_____

_____

_____

_____

_____

_____

_____

_____

_____

_____

_____

_____

_____

_____

_____

_____

_____

DAY 5

My heart has been my biggest enemy for as long as I can remember. My heart has kept me in places that I knew no longer served me. It has caused me to go against myself and even my family and friends at one point. It has kept my vision cloudy, my voice silenced, and my ears muffled to the truth of many things.

Being able to grow myself when it came to emotional intelligence changed how I view myself and how I conduct myself with others. Not only being conscious of what I am feeling, but also being able to locate the root cause. Navigating the loss of my daughter has taught me that grief shows up in sadness, fear, anger, frustration, exhaustion, and even in excitement or extreme happiness. And all are totally normal.

As humans we will experience many emotions triggered by past experiences, new experiences, and just general day to day life. Due to many traumatic things in my past, I was able to recognize that my primary emotion was disgust. I was unhappy with me, unhappy with things around me, and unhappy about being unhappy. Through therapy and self-work I discovered that the disgust emotion was based off how I saw myself and how I processed the things that had and were happening in my life. The constant feeling of not being enough, anxiety, fear, regret, disappointed all became squatters in my mind taking up residency in my heart without permission. Without a doubt causing turmoil in my mind, body, and my spirit. Ask yourself how am I feeling? Allow yourself time to process what you are really feeling and why? When things are quiet around you what do you feel ? If you find that your primary emotion is negative based emotion seek out the root cause. What you find is that the primary emotion that you have ties directly to how you operate in your life , the choices you make, the places you go, the people you entertain, and even the foods that you eat. I encourage you today to stop searching in the branches for what only can be found in the roots. Once we can bring to the light the things that keep us shackled in the darkness, we then can find gratitude in all things daily. Not because everything is perfect, but because God is still God no matter what may come.

"The purposes of a person's heart are deep waters, but one who has insight draws them out." **-Proverbs 20:5**

"Be still, and know that I am God." **-Psalms 46:10**

Today's Reflection

M T W Th F S Su   Date: _____

What is your primary emotion from day to day?

_____
_____
_____
_____
_____
_____
_____
_____
_____
_____
_____
_____
_____
_____
_____
_____
_____
_____
_____
_____
_____

DAY 6

Alone??!!! What's that, you may ask. Many of us wear so many hats that we don't always get the luxury of solitude. Or we choose to constantly place ourselves around others due to the uncomfortable feelings that being alone comes with at times. If you don't like being with you... why would anyone else like being with you? The person you should love hanging out with the most should be yourself. When was the last time you took yourself to dinner and enjoyed you? Played some music and just danced and laughed to yourself? How do you take care of you?

As a mother of four, at that time, I remember working overtime to make sure that my girls had everything they needed and even some of what they wanted. I would be out anywhere and would see something and immediately pick it up for them without a second thought. In the same store, I would see something that I liked, only to pick it up and carry it around the store, and by the time I get to the register, ask them to put it back. I would have 101 reasons why I did not need it. I literally reinforced the behavior to put myself last daily. I didn't have any clothes, never splurged on hair or nails, meals, make up, perfume, nothing at all. Then to add insult to injury, the man I had been dating would constantly compare me to other women, as if he didn't see me sacrificing myself so that our children could have.

Yet, God is always strategic. He created connections that helped me find a balance without feeling guilty. I met other women who were mothers and they consistently invested into their personal appearance and other extracurricular activities. They helped me understand that doing something for myself was not needed, but required. If you are connected to people who are only open to be poured into but can't pour back into you, you will end up empty. The moments when you take care of yourself allow you to reset & refocus to continue on your journey. The assignments in your life require you to be at your best to do the work that God is calling you to do. Find time to be in the presence of God daily with no distractions. Find time to be with yourself daily. See how that time manifests more acceptance, grace, and peace in all the other areas of your life.

"Very early in the morning, while it was still dark, Jesus got up, left the house and went off to a solitary place, where he prayed." **-Mark 1:35**

Today's Reflection

M T W Th F S Su   Date: _____

What does taking care of YOU look and feel like?

_____
_____
_____
_____
_____
_____
_____
_____
_____
_____
_____
_____
_____
_____
_____
_____
_____
_____
_____
_____
_____

DAY 7

Transitioning from being a teenager and living with my parents to being a new mother and living with a boyfriend was drastic. The whole thing seemed to happen overnight. Moving from a stage in life that your autonomy was managed by your parents to a stage in life where your responsibilities and relationship controlled your autonomy would leave anyone in state of confusion and lost. For the majority of my life I was conditioned to put the needs of others before my own needs. What I was trained to believe is what I needed was not important and putting my needs in front of others was selfish. I was led to believe that if I prioritized myself that meant I was a being bad mother, girlfriend, friend, or employee. When the truth was, being aware of your needs would have aided in fostering better relationships, personal growth, and key factors to managing self care.

When I was able to identify what I needed from others, it also allowed me to see what I needed from myself and GOD. One of the things that I needed was the reassurance to be me, not perfect just me. What I need from God is just grace, because as I am growing I tend to be rebellious. I know you said go down the road but let me see where this road goes God. I'm sure He gets sick of me, but the awesome thing about God and the people that He will connect you to on this journey, is that they will be equipped with the capacity and the grace to give you what you need and to direct you.

"He restores my soul. He leads me in paths of righteousness for his name's sake." **-Psalms 23:3 NKJV**

"He renews my strength. He guides me along right paths, bringing honor to his name." **-Psalms 23:3 NLT**

Today's Reflection

M T W Th F S Su

Date: _____

What are you needing the most? What are you needing from God?

_____
_____
_____
_____
_____
_____
_____
_____
_____
_____
_____
_____
_____
_____
_____
_____
_____
_____
_____
_____
_____
_____
_____

DAY 8

Since I can remember I have always felt like I was not smart enough, not pretty enough, not cool enough, just not enough of anything. For that reason, I isolated myself although I always desired authentic connections. However, due to past experiences, when I felt like I was totally authentic people deemed me as too much. I crave validation from others, I operate at 80% authenticity in fear of being too much, and I somehow can never find and give the grace that I give to others to myself. Today, stand firm that even in the midst of it all, you are enough and you will never be too much for purposeful connections. We have to be mindful of what we expose our mind, eye, and ear gates to because that is either going to further the negative narrative or dispel it.

Let's do what I call the 555 Challenge. Take 5 minutes right now, look in the mirror and say these 5 things aloud:

1) Accomplishments & Successes (ex: *Today I got a good mark on a test*)
2) Risks Taken (e.g., I stood up for a kid being bullied)
3) Disciplines Kept (e.g., I did my homework)
4) Temptations Resisted
5) Most beautiful attributes

Follow with 5 affirmations

"But he said to me, "My grace is sufficient for you, for my power is made perfect in weakness." Therefore I will boast all the more gladly about my weaknesses, so that Christ's power may rest on me. That is why, for Christ's sake, I delight in weaknesses, in insults, in hardships, in persecutions, in difficulties. For when I am weak, then I am strong."

-2 Corinthians 12:9-10

Today's Reflection

M T W Th F S Su   Date: _____

Have you felt like you are not good enough or that you were too much?

_____

_____

_____

_____

_____

_____

_____

_____

_____

_____

_____

_____

_____

_____

_____

_____

_____

_____

_____

_____

_____

_____

DAY 9

Hard truth is realizing that what God has for you has absolutely nothing to do with what He is doing in someone else's life. When we are hyper focused on what others have or are doing, we create a spirit of doubt, jealousy, and envy that the enemy uses to keep us stagnant and out of God's will. With the day and age of social media it's so easy to feel like you are not doing enough, not beautiful enough, rich enough, that you are behind the mark. For the majority of my life, I suffered with insecurities not being able to see the beauty within myself due to constantly comparing myself to others. I didn't fully understand that people typically only show their highlights and never show you the full picture. We become addicted to false perfection via filters & photoshop, fueled by illusions and encompassed with ego, greed, and envy. We are so consumed with the grass being greener on the other side that we miss the signs that it's Astroturf.

The truth of the matter is that you were created to be YOU! Everything that you are, and everything you are called to be is already in you. There is no need to attempt to compare or adjust who you are. What God has shown me is that my flaws and hardships are what He will use to heal others. I don't need to be like anyone else. I don't need to cover my weaknesses, or imperfections. True courage and confidence comes with accepting yourself where you are, and trusting the process of purpose. Starting now, stop watching others, and trust that God a plan for you. Talk with God and ask Him to show you what success for you looks like in Him, and remove your own ideas of success so that you can better align with God's purpose. No longer let comparison kidnap your courage, confidence, joy, and peace by denouncing that spirit of comparison. There is WIN for you in God's kingdom, stop comparing your WHEN to the wins of others.

"Have I not commanded you? Be strong and of good courage; do not be afraid, nor be dismayed, for the Lord your God is with you wherever you go." **-Joshua 1:9**

Today's Reflection

M T W Th F S Su   Date: _____

How has comparison kidnapped your courage and confidence?

_____
_____
_____
_____
_____
_____
_____
_____
_____
_____
_____
_____
_____
_____
_____
_____
_____
_____
_____
_____
_____
_____
_____
_____

Many times, on this journey called life, we don't always recognize the things that are the roots that keep affecting the fruits that we bare. I never really understood a lot of my reactions. I thought they were just consistent ways that I handled situations that were familiar. After many years of repeated behavior, it took me seeking counseling and learning to sit with myself to see me. Yes, I was resilient, strong, forward-thinking, and thoughtful, but these were all overdeveloped strengths. I didn't like to ask for help because of previous experiences. In the past, when I asked for help, the responses I received from people made me never want to have to ask for help again. I hated that feeling. I also used to overextend myself because I knew what it felt like not to have help. Not to mention many unresolved traumas with my mother & father that constantly showed up in all my relationships. This all led my mind to become a giant ball of "stay way over there away from everyone and do this all on your own".

What God showed me was that there are times when we have to go back before we can be called forward. I had to go back to the places that caused injury and upset me before I could walk into the places He ordained for the healed version of me. I encourage you today to find the strength to revisit places that you've attempted to disregard. Those places only have power over us if we try to avoid them. Yet if we have enough courage, we can find peace, compassion, understanding, empathy, and direction. Think about it this way, ...what if your childhood experiences were the foundation to your purpose? What if, in order to stay in alignment, break generational curses, and experience growth, there is a level of understanding, forgiveness, and grace needed for others that changes the entire essence of your mind and your revelation of who God is calling you to be?

Today's Reflection

M T W Th F S Su   Date: _____

What are you carrying from childhood that is affecting you now in adulthood?

_____

_____

_____

_____

_____

_____

_____

_____

_____

_____

_____

_____

_____

_____

_____

_____

_____

_____

_____

_____

_____

_____

_____

DAY 11

What's stopping you from being the greater version of yourself? The top 3 things on my list of many, yes I said many, would be inconsistency, familiarity, and control. Inconsistency is the predator of all achievements and dreams. I am what I like to call consistently inconsistent. Many times we put so much emphasis on starting. We say things like, "Start somewhere," or "Just start today." And there's nothing wrong with those statements, but we must not forget the importance of finishing. God requires that we give Him not only trust, but He requires us to trust Him consistently: which requires obedience! As I have grown in God, I realized that my lack of obedience in one season caused undue suffering in the next. It's imperative to stay consistent in seeking God's words and voice as He propels you towards what you have been called for.

Now on to familiarity. This was a struggle for most of my life. I love to plant and sometimes re-plant myself in familiar places. God had told me to move and I was like, "No! It's not even that bad. Imma stay a lil bit." Telling you this is embarrassing, but it's very true. We can't be so loyal to old habits, places, people, and things that we forfeit our future. God will deliver you from the places that no longer serve you, but you have to trust Him to get you there through the uncharted territories. Yes, its scary and uncomfortable and this is where my 3rd thing reared its ugly head CONTROL. Imagine asking God I need to know A through G before I go. (I can see the blank stare on His face. lol) God will order your steps but he has the game plan. Will you surrender to his perfect leadership ? I was so focused on getting to the PROMISE that I attempted to skip the PROCESS. There are somethings that God has to pull out of you so that you can be impactful in his Kingdom. Don't be afraid of exposure or people seeing you struggle . This is how you are stretched and become strong in God. As you are being birthed for new purpose its going to require you to let go of old thinking, old habits, old reactions, and old versions of yourself. New life requires death in the areas that are not conducive to creating a new version of yourself. Mourn and move on to purpose.

"For we are his workmanship, created in Christ Jesus for good works, which God prepared beforehand, that we should walk in them."

-Ephesians 2:10

Today's Reflection

M T W Th F S Su   Date: _____

What things in your past do you struggle with that's stopping you from being a greater version of yourself?

_____
_____
_____
_____
_____
_____
_____
_____
_____
_____
_____
_____
_____
_____
_____
_____
_____
_____
_____
_____
_____

DAY 12

There is no one like you. When you were created, you were specifically molded with a mission that only you can fulfill. For years I asked God for clarity of what my purpose was, assuming that it was to be a mother. That was a role that I would take on as I operated in my purpose, but was my purpose bigger than my household? I spent so many years looking for clues outside of myself including assuming roles and comparing myself to others. When the truth is, all I needed to do was just accept and agree that God has preordained me for His work on this earth, and that is what reveals the steps to His destiny for us. Imagine literally taking one way every day and just saying its has to be a better way for me to get there. And BOOM steps appear!! and the more you focus on believing bigger more steps appear until you arrive at the location. By doing this you have to Trust God will make the step as solid as the one before, it is going to require that you be uncomfortably available, relinquish the need to control, and see YOU how God sees you.

I recall being engulfed in so much chaos at times from home life, relationships, habits, and work. I was like, "God ain't no way you expect me to help someone else, I am barely making it myself." What God showed me was that in the places I struggled, and was attacked the most by the enemy, were also the places that God intended to use me. I started being connected to people that I could pour into just as others did for me. It was in my inadequacy that God gave me sufficient purpose. Everything you have encountered has been designed specifically for your purpose in God's kingdom. All you need is curiosity, courage, and commitment. What are your gifts? What ways have you impacted others?

"And we know that in all things God works for the good of those who love him, who have been called according to his purpose." **-Romans 8:28**

Today's Reflection

M T W Th F S Su   Date: _____

What is distinctive about you? What are you being called to do?

_____

_____

_____

_____

_____

_____

_____

_____

_____

_____

_____

_____

_____

_____

_____

_____

_____

_____

_____

_____

_____

_____

DAY 13

An emotion that I tried for years to avoid was peace. I know you are thinking why would you do that? Because waking up to a good day felt scary to me, and here is why... February 8, 2021, I woke up and took my twins to school. I saw my older set of twins before they left the house to get on the bus. I took a shower, brushed my teeth, and I went to the DMV to get the title of the car I just bought for my 2nd oldest. I was told something was missing. I went to pick up the missing document, then drove back to the DMV to finish the process which was surprisingly quick. I stopped by the dollar store to get a bow so that I could surprise her when she returned home from a trip with the car. I got myself ready for work, and then the kid's dad called me and said, "You talked to Kiya? They say she has been shot." I replied, "No, I haven't." He then shattered my world when he said, "They say she's dead."

I immediately replied, "Huh?" Not because I didn't hear him, but because it just wasn't registering or making any sense. I hung up and began to call my friend who worked in law enforcement to see if she had heard anything. I tried to reach out to people who would know her whereabouts. I just sat down in confusion and was overcome with disbelief, replaying what I just heard, and in complete loss of direction on which way to go. I got a call from her oldest brother, and asked if he knew, and he told me the place and that he believed it was true! I grabbed my keys, got in my car and started to drive. I don't recall the drive. I just recall my phone ringing with loved ones asking questions that I had no answer to. I just knew I needed to get there. I hoped that it was wrong that there was confusion. I got to the apartment complex in Greer, SC and I ran up only to be stopped. I asked what happened and if my daughter was ok. I explained who I was and they said that she had been shot and killed.

I asked to see her because I couldn't believe it. I needed to see for myself before I could believe the nightmare was true. I was told they were processing the scene and to go home and someone would come to my home to talk with me. But I couldn't leave. I couldn't see who was under the white cloth. I needed to know. I needed to see.

I asked for a chair and I sat out there for hours in the cold waiting for them to finish, just staring at the cloth that covered the body. Hours passed and I just stared no words, no nothing, just sitting and waiting. Each time I looked up more and more family members gathered. Different detectives attempted to start conversations, but my mind was too far away to even comprehend. I just needed to see. Finally the Coroner arrived and I begged please I need to know for myself if it's her. They agreed, the Coroner pulled back the sheet that had been covering her the entire time. I will never forget her eyes, open and so far away. It was her... she was indeed gone.

The wave of the realness of the loss swept through my body, dropping me to my knees. I felt my heartbreak and sheer agony engulf every part of me. The floodgates of other emotions like shock, guilt, disbelief, failure, sadness, hopelessness, and shame tumbled in like a tsunami. My daughter, my heart, my 1st love, my friend, my right hand was gone. The most devastating painstaking day that I never wanted to experience, there was nothing about the day that told me it would end like that. I didn't wake up feeling doom or dread, nothing fell off the wall to indicate an issue, no dreams, no number sequences, no nothing... it was a good day like any other, or so I thought.

I'm a mother. Where was the intuition?? Did I miss it? I am a believer in God. Did I miss it? I'm a woman. How did I not know?

The day started out as a good day but changed my life forever... which is why peaceful days scared me. Until recently, it was easier to choose or create chaos and live it. Because if something goes wrong it's expected and would make sense. Yet God reminded me that the battle with the enemy begins in the mind before you see it anywhere else. The emotions we avoid are very often connected to places of pain that we have or still may be experiencing. Trust God, that whatever was meant to break you, God is restoring you better than before. That doesn't always include understanding. I will never understand why my daughter was taken, but I have learned to accept the purpose in the pain. What do you avoid and what is tied to that emotion?

"But for those who are righteous, the way is not steep and rough. You are a God who does what is right, and you smooth out the path ahead of them."

-Isaiah 26:7

Today's Reflection

M T W Th F S Su   Date: _____

What emotions do you try to avoid? Why?

_____
_____
_____
_____
_____
_____
_____
_____
_____
_____
_____
_____
_____
_____
_____
_____
_____
_____
_____
_____
_____
_____
_____

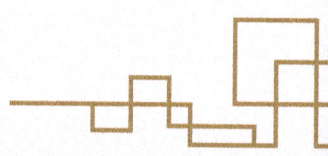

Today's Reflection

M T W Th F S Su   Date: _____

Continued...

_____
_____
_____
_____
_____
_____
_____
_____
_____
_____
_____
_____
_____
_____
_____
_____
_____
_____
_____
_____
_____
_____
_____
_____
_____
_____
_____

DAY 14

When I was in school, they taught us about cognitive dissonance. However, they never really focused on how pivotal those moments are when it comes to the trajectory of your life paths. I experienced this moment not too long ago with a man that I now understand was a mirror. I knew this man would do anything for me, but he was also capable of doing anything to me. I felt like he loved me, but very much hated me in the same way. He was a safe place that wasn't too safe. Seems like a pretty easy choice, huh? Lose myself trying to love him... or choose me with the loss of him. He came into my life when I didn't love me. He possessed some good qualities as a man, but due to his trauma, he truly didn't have the capacity to love me. How can you give something you never truly experienced? Yet I found myself giving him love, patience, grace, good energy, all the things that I thought I would never possess again. Yet, there it was, and although he had some surefire red flags, He was also a preview of many of the things I desired in a man. The truth is that somewhere in the attempts to navigate his brokenness, I uncovered my brokenness.

What I realized is that when we think we're broken, we think we just have to get all the pieces and put them back together. But, there is power in being broken because you get to leave out the pieces that you no longer need and the ones that no longer fit who you are becoming. By sorting through the shattered shards of who you once were, you get to keep the pieces that fit to the new you and discard all the pieces that don't. You'll no longer run the risk of constantly cutting yourself on misfit pieces and accidentally bleeding on others. It's about embracing who you are becoming, the version of you that God has already called you to be. God unlocks new levels of us through experiences. Learning to rest safely in God's words and arms has changed my life completely. So I ask you, what does your safe place look and feel like?

"Whoever dwells in the shelter of the Most High will rest in the shadow of the Almighty. [I will say of the Lord, "He is my refuge and my fortress, my God, in whom I trust. Surely he will save you from the fowler's snare and from the deadly pestilence." **-Psalms 91:1-3**

Today's Reflection

M T W Th F S Su

Date: _____

What does a safe place look & feel like to you ?

_____
_____
_____
_____
_____
_____
_____
_____
_____
_____
_____
_____
_____
_____
_____
_____
_____
_____
_____
_____
_____
_____

DAY 15

Betrayal and disappointment seem to be two key learning elements from the beginning of time. They go hand-in-hand at times or they can pair with other emotions just as easily. At times, I get so angry when I look at moments when I felt betrayed, whether it was with family, friends, spouses, or even at work. Then, I think if they betrayed Jesus, why would I be exempt from the betrayal?

No matter who you are, what you have, or who you may know, people will disappoint you at some point. There are times when the violation is intentional and other times when it may not be. Lack of intention doesn't make the hurt, betrayal, or disappointment less painful; nor does that always mean that someone else's action is a direct reflection of who you are. What I learned is that God will use betrayal to reveal when we may need to change direction or grow spiritually. Think about the times when God has shown you on several occasions, that many of the connections we cling to are not purposeful connections. Yet, we stay connected, and many times we fall out of alignment and don't even know it. I internalized betrayal and disappointment so deeply that I began to believe that everything that people had done to betray or disappoint me was my fault.

As I reflected, I learned that God's plan was always bigger than the betrayal. The times that I experienced heartache due to betrayal and disappointment caused me to seek him more. I was surprised that when I sought Him in these moments, I found forgiveness for the ones that hurt me, the capacity to pray and keep myself open to purposeful connections, and the ability to sip on the sweetness of life vs binge drink bitterness. There is a purpose and plan to God's way of revealing others to us, while using the situation to prepare for what's next. I'm thankful for the clarity, course adjustments, strength, purpose, forgiveness, and discernment that I found in the midst of betrayal and disappointment.

"For I know the plans I have for you," declares the LORD, *"plans to prosper you and not to harm you, plans to give you hope and a future."*
                                                          -Jeremiah 29:11

Today's Reflection

M T W Th F S Su   Date: _____

How has betrayal and disappointment plagued your spirit, mind, and relationships? What blessing did God reveal to you in those moments?

_____

_____

_____

_____

_____

_____

_____

_____

_____

_____

_____

_____

_____

_____

_____

_____

_____

_____

_____

_____

DAY 16

I once was told that what the devil can't destroy, he distracts. Distractions from God's voice, purpose, and blessings have shown up in many forms. I've seen this mostly through sheer disobedience, but also through poor connections, achievements, finances, social media, laziness, and family. It never fails that as God is calling me closer, the enemy sends me a distraction in the form of discourse with my family, a man, problems, or a surplus of opportunities. My mind is so heavy with the stress from what is going on in my home that I can't focus. If it's not that, I'm entertaining a man, problem after problem, or I have 100 new ideas and things that I want to do. Mind is everywhere except what God has told me to do.

Being able to be steadfast in the word of God as He births you into greater can be difficult with so many distractions. As God is calling you to the next level, it requires focus and obedience. God has given you a purpose, and you have a calling on your life. As you are growing in God, the enemy will begin to throw so many things your way to get you to become out of alignment. Even procrastination is a form of disobedience because delayed obedience is still disobedience. Pairing disobedience with arrogance that God will give you tomorrow to do what He told you to do today has a huge impact on your blessing. I know we want to think, "Oh yeah, God, just remove the distractions," but as God is attempting to advance you in His Kingdom, there will also be opposition. God will never act as a component competing against the many distractions we choose.

Today, I encourage you to sit with God. Ask what His vision is for your life. Does His vision align with what you are doing? Is there anything that God has told you to do that you haven't done? Remember that wherever your interest and focus are, that is where you multiply. Where is your interest? What's keeping you distracted?

"The LORD replied, "Don't say, 'I'm too young,' for you must go wherever I send you and say whatever I tell you." **-Jeremiah 1:7 NLT**

Today's Reflection

M   T   W   Th   F   S   Su   Date: _____

How do distractions affect you? What needs are being met by your distractions? What's the underlining unmet need?

_____
_____
_____
_____
_____
_____
_____
_____
_____
_____
_____
_____
_____
_____
_____
_____
_____
_____
_____
_____
_____
_____
_____
_____

DAY 17

Disruption is defined as a disturbance or problem that interrupts an event, activity, or process. We all experience bouts of interruption as we journey throughout life. Many times, disruptions in our lives feel like a burden or nuisance. When in actuality, God uses those moments of disruption to realign us. Very often, before the disruptions, God has made several attempts to get your attention to elevate you to a new level of self, or just to get you to be still. For me, God has used a variety of disruptions from connections, finances, health, and even death to align me with who He has called me to be. Disappointment at times can be used by the enemy to attack your faith and generate fear or anxiety. Just remember God is the Alpha & the Omega, which means He is never taken aback by the things that are taking place. The goal is for you to trust in Him fully, no matter what it may look or feel like. It's important that as He begins to shift you to a higher identity that you are not so loyal to who you currently are that you miss who God is calling you to be. Understanding that His ways are better than your own, and not allowing a viewpoint to override God's provision. We just have to change how we see trials. Ask yourself, is this to learn something, shift me, birth me, or simply bring me back into God's presence?

"These have come so that the proven genuineness of your faith—of greater worth than gold, which perishes even though refined by fire—may result in praise, glory and honor when Jesus Christ is revealed. Though you have not seen him, you love him; and even though you do not see him now, you believe in him and are filled with an inexpressible and glorious joy, for you are receiving the end result of your faith, the salvation of your souls."

Today's Reflection

M   T   W   Th   F   S   Su   Date: _____

How has God used disruption to realign you with His purpose?

_____

_____

_____

_____

_____

_____

_____

_____

_____

_____

_____

_____

_____

_____

_____

_____

_____

_____

_____

_____

_____

_____

_____

_____

DAY 18

Grief has had a major impact on my life. I lost my mother when I was 22 and my father at age 26, so the journey to my 30s just seemed shrouded in misfortune, sadness, and loss. I was grieving the loss of my parents, feeling the loss of support and direction. I was grieving the loss of myself because by that age, I was a mother of 4. I had the worries of what seemed like the world on my shoulders. I was carrying the loss of my parents while also trying to navigate the complicated grief behind my mother's death. It all seemed to keep me in a state of complacency, fear, and silence. I fought through that because I did not want my trying to cope with life to affect my children, and I was tired of being quiet. Only to get to age 39 and to truly believe that I have this life thing figured out, and my daughter Zakiya is murdered at 19. The heartache of burying anyone you love is hard by itself, the sheer heartbreak, disbelief, and complete brokenness that occurred when I had to bury my child will forever be unexplainable. I know that 02/08/2021 shattered me.

I have spent the last 3 years trying to piece myself back together to even a shell of who I thought I was. I was in a state of mind where I wanted to remove myself from everyone and everybody. I operated in fear, tolerating behaviors because, "What if?" I used people and things to fill the voids of sadness, keeping myself busy, and overaccountability. So when I look back and say, "Oh, I overcame grief," no, that's not true. I'm still here, managing it day by day. I survived what was surely designed to take me out. YES, I DID, but at what cost? I survived grief in a sense, but I didn't win. I lost peace, I lost faith, I lost time, I lost my purpose, I lost boundaries, I lost confidence, I lost interest, I lost joy, I lost laughs, I lost time. I guess you think well, man, there's no hope for me. Yet it was all necessary; it's so easy to focus on what was lost that we miss what was gained. What you lost will forever be important. I wish I had a map for smoother navigation.

I do not have that map, and it's ok for you to feel however you feel. I encourage you today to look for what you gained in your grief. I lost my daughter, my friend, my confidante. I gained the ability to see myself, the realization that in my brokenness, with my knee bloody and bowed, tears running from my eyes, that God saw me and when I thought He left me, He was with me sorting through the shatter. Helping me see what needs to be removed and adding what's missing. God told me you will never be the same. There is purpose in the pain, there is clarity in the calamity, there is wholeness with the brokenness. Grief changes our hearts, minds, bodies, and spirits. Yet the world tells us that in those moments we are closer to God than ever. Acknowledge how grief has changed you, good and bad. And ask God for the vision. Grief keeps us stagnant, hard, sad, angry, and out of the will of God. We have limited control over the losses that we experience, but with God, we can navigate those losses purposefully.

"The Lord is close to the brokenhearted and saves those who are crushed in spirit." **-Psalm 34:18**

Today's Reflection

M   T   W   Th   F   S   Su   Date: _____

How has grief changed you?

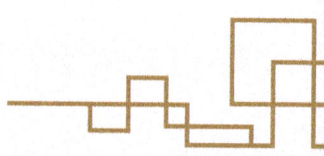

Today's Reflection

M   T   W   Th   F   S   Su   Date: _____

Continued...

_____
_____
_____
_____
_____
_____
_____
_____
_____
_____
_____
_____
_____
_____
_____
_____
_____
_____
_____
_____
_____
_____
_____

DAY 19

Forgiveness, at times, feels like a foreign concept. Depending on the wounds we carry, a lack of forgiveness can feel like a safe place where we are protected from being hurt. The truth is that the lack of forgiveness for others, and most importantly, ourselves, only stops us from evolving and elevating. There are things that have occurred in my life that I have immense amounts of anger about, yet I know God understands. His word tells us "Be angry and do not sin; do not let the sun go down on your anger, and give no opportunity to the devil" Ephesians 4:26-2. It's not that someone did not hurt or betray you, or that the disappointment or pain is not real. What matters is how we respond to it. Did the angry feelings or lack of forgiveness change our hearts? Do you feel out of alignment? Did your vision change? I was 40 years old before I was able to gift myself forgiveness. I woke up one morning, wrote a list of the things that I felt I needed to forgive myself for.

- Worrying about how others see me VS how God sees me- It's just not your concern what others think or feel about you. God sees our hearts and knows our minds. The only thing that matters is your heart staying clean and your mind remaining steadfast on Him.

- Desensitizing mistreatment- I buried my feelings for so long, being able to forgive others for their trespasses against me by watering down the hurt I suffered. Being so understanding of others, and intolerant when it came to my flaws.

- No boundaries - Understanding that my lack of boundaries was never because I didn't care about myself, but because I never had the autonomy to choose me for many reasons stemming from childhood. Many times, we choose others over ourselves, not because we don't love ourselves, but because we are not aware of our options to choose something different.

- Hyper responsibility - Everything is not on me, I can't control everything.

- Staying in places too long / Returning to uninhabitable places - Fear and familiarity are a powerful duo. It's so easy to stay or go back, we at times confuse endurance with strength. I endured extensive seasons of stagnation because I confused the two. I understand that we have to learn to mourn, move, and trust God for the new. What we want is not always what God has for us.

- Being quiet - If speaking my truth shifts the atmosphere, it was a necessary shift & I'm ok with that.

- Not loving God & myself more - When you asked about your 1st love, are you trying to remember the person's name from 6th grade? Is it God? Is it yourself? Falling in love with God is where I found the love I needed for myself.

- Worrying about the why- Why is a rabbit hole that keeps you focused on the problem - instead, I'm focused on the what (needs to be done), how (it needs to be done), and when (to execute). Trust God.

"Believing-prayer will heal you, and Jesus will put you on your feet. And if you've sinned, you'll be forgiven - healed inside and out." **-James 5:15**

Today's Reflection

M   T   W   Th   F   S   Su   Date: _____

When was the last time you forgave yourself and what do you need to forgive yourself for now?

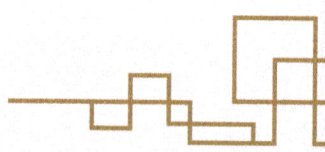

_____
_____
_____
_____
_____
_____
_____
_____
_____
_____
_____
_____
_____
_____
_____
_____
_____
_____
_____
_____
_____
_____

Today's Reflection

M T W Th F S Su

Date: _____

Continued...

_____

_____

_____

_____

_____

_____

_____

_____

_____

_____

_____

_____

_____

_____

_____

_____

_____

_____

_____

_____

_____

_____

DAY 20

I feel that people think that others self-sabotage on purpose when really, I think that it manifests in thinking as a "safe alternative" driven by trauma, need for control, and many other factors. For me, it has been staying and returning to the familiar, whether it was a relationship, a job, or toxic behaviors. I was literally settling for the bad because it was at least something. Ridiculous, I know, but as I began to visit the unhealed places deep within, my expectations began to change, and it was a daily fight not to settle for just anything any longer. Healing and self-sabotage are two interconnected concepts that often go hand in hand. Healing refers to the process of recovering and finding inner balance after experiencing emotional, mental, or physical challenges. It involves addressing and resolving the underlying issues that contribute to our pain or difficulties. On the other hand, self-sabotage refers to the unconscious behaviors, thoughts, or actions that hinder our progress, growth, and overall well-being. It is often driven by deep-seated fears, limiting beliefs, or unresolved traumas. Self-sabotage can manifest in various ways, such as procrastination, self-criticism, negative self-talk, or engaging in harmful behaviors. The relationship between healing and self-sabotage is complex. While healing requires self-awareness, self-reflection, and taking constructive steps towards growth, self-sabotage can sabotage these efforts by undermining our confidence, creating self-doubt, or triggering self-destructive behaviors. Recognizing and addressing self-sabotaging patterns is crucial for effective healing. It involves identifying the underlying fears or beliefs that drive self-sabotage and replacing them with empowering thoughts and behaviors. This may require seeking support from therapists, coaches, or engaging in self-help practices like mindfulness, journaling, or affirmations. Ultimately, the journey of healing and overcoming self-sabotage is unique to each individual. It requires patience, self-compassion, and a commitment to personal growth. By understanding and addressing self-sabotaging patterns, we can create a healthier and more fulfilling life.

"The wise woman builds her house, but the foolish pulls it down with her hands." **-Proverbs 14:1**

Today's Reflection

M   T   W   Th   F   S   Su

Date: _____

In what ways do you self-sabotage?

_____

_____

_____

_____

_____

_____

_____

_____

_____

_____

_____

_____

_____

_____

_____

_____

_____

_____

_____

_____

_____

_____

DAY 21

Gratitude is defined as an emotion of the heart, excited by a favor or benefit received; a sentiment of kindness or goodwill towards a benefactor; thankfulness. But what does gratitude mean and look like to you? How often do you come into God's presence with just gratitude? So many times I found myself talking about what I don't have or what I want, without showing thankfulness for all that I do have. When I look back, I can recall a time when a lot of what I have now were things that seemed unreachable, and almost impossible. It's so easy to complain about all the things we experience on a day-to-day basis, but I encourage you not to let God's favor become so familiar that you stop showing your gratitude. Today and every day, practice a gratitude adjustment, not just saying simple thank you Lord, but also feeling in your heart and giving in return. I used to get caught up in "fixing" everything so I could be at peace, and what God showed me was that my mindset was the door to unlocking peace and blessings. In life, there are going to be trials and tribulations that we have to endure. As we endure the storms, we must think of gratitude as an umbrella, surgeon, shield, and ATM, shielding us from the pain. Think of gratitude as a surgeon restoring our joy so that we can continue our journey, a shield protecting us from the enemy's plots, and an ATM dispensing God's favor over our future. What if the keys to unlocking the next level of your purpose are not so much about preparing for the future, but what if it's about finding gratitude in everything good, bad, and in between?

"Do not be anxious about anything, but in everything by prayer and supplication with thanksgiving let your requests be made known to God." **-Philippians 4:6**

Today's Reflection

M T W Th F S Su   Date: _____

Make a gratitude list. What are you thankful for?

_____

_____

_____

_____

_____

_____

_____

_____

_____

_____

_____

_____

_____

_____

_____

_____

_____

_____

_____

_____

_____

_____

_____

_____

_____

DAY 22

Authenticity is defined as being true to one's own personality, spirit, or character. So what does the authentic version of you look and feel like? It is very easy, with the influence of social media and friends, to allow others to define authenticity. When the truth is that it can only be defined by you. If the authentic version of you is guarded, or silly, fearful, or even just plain out mean, then that's ok. Being authentic is not about being the BEST version of you, it's about being just you, the best and the worst. It's understanding that there is more work to be done and not holding yourself in a chokehold because of the worst.

Being authentic and healing are closely connected. When we are authentic, we are true to ourselves and express our thoughts, feelings, and experiences honestly. This allows us to connect with others on a deeper level and build genuine relationships where we can acknowledge and accept our emotions, traumas, and vulnerabilities. This self-awareness and acceptance are essential for healing and personal growth. Being authentic allows us to let go of pretenses and masks, enabling us to address our wounds and work through them. It creates an environment of trust, both within ourselves and in our relationships, which is necessary for healing to occur. Keep in mind that the authentic version of you is constantly growing. So today, decide who you are, who you want to be, and what that looks and feels like to you. Don't allow anyone else to place the authentic standards on you... because if you conform to what authenticity looks like for someone else... Are you really being authentic???

Today's Reflection

M T W Th F S Su

Date: _____

What does being authentic look like to you?

_____

_____

_____

_____

_____

_____

_____

_____

_____

_____

_____

_____

_____

_____

_____

_____

_____

_____

_____

_____

_____

_____

_____

DAY 23

When we think about the people we choose to connect to in life I have not always made the best choices. I never really thought about the huge impact that making the decisions of who we become friends, date, or choose to do business with affects our destiny. It wasn't until I got older I realized that I desired connections but often settled for attachments. By doing this I found myself in places that provided me just enough light to stay alive but never enough to really grow. My growth or my success at times was such a threat that it would be an all hands mission to stunt it.

As I started to experience real shifts in my life, I would always be in a state of shock when God would remove people that I felt were supposed to be there for my entire journey. In the beginning I would fight so hard, God would remove, I would go back and pick them back up. I'm sure at this time and very many times with me this is when god would give me the blank stare like, "Girl!" What I learned the hard way is that when we fail to be obedient, trust God, and separate from certain people in one season, that they usually cause suffering or heartache in the seasons to come. There is just no way to arrive at your purpose while holding on to the wrong individuals. There is such a calling on my life that the devil desires so badly to destroy me but he can't, so what he has done in the past is to keep distracted and confused in my mind to keep me delayed. So, I ask you who are you connected to? When we think of hoarding we think of hoarding we thing of things, but some us hoard people. Are there some people in your life that are blocking you from what God has for you? Is my relationship mutually beneficial?

Do they align with not just who you are, but who you are becoming? Do they pour into just as you pour into them? Ask God to send you purposeful connections. Why? Because maybe the reason nothing seems to be going in your favor is because God will not place you in a winning position, because the people you connected to will cause you to waste it.

"Walk with the wise and become wise, for a companion of fools suffers harm." **-Proverbs 13:20**

Today's Reflection

M T W Th F S Su   Date: _____

Are your personal relationships mutually beneficial?

_____
_____
_____
_____
_____
_____
_____
_____
_____
_____
_____
_____
_____
_____
_____
_____
_____
_____
_____
_____
_____
_____
_____
_____

DAY 24

Being a people pleaser has made me my own worst enemy. I have constantly gone, not only against myself, but against God worried about what other people would think of me if I say no, if I don't show up, if I say what I really feel. What I realized is that doing for others and expecting the same only sets you up for disappointment. In many of my relationships from business, so called friends, and even spouses I have found myself that doing what's best for the other person even if it hurts me, causes me some type of inconvenience, or to feel some kind of way. It's a hard cycle to break free from, especially when you genuinely want to be there for people because you know what it feels like for no one to show up or look out for you. However, almost every time I find myself in the same cycles, same hurts, same feelings. The lessons teach you to choose you and trust God. People who really love you and care for you wont make you feel like reciprocity has to be forced. One thing that's always been said is that people will show you who they are, and believe them. The first time anyone shows any lack of appreciation, respect, loyalty, or just sheer weirdness, set a boundary right then and protect your space. Of course we are all human and we all make mistakes, there will be times when you need to show grace. What I will say is the ones that are deserving of grace, will show two things: accountability and changed behavior. I let my need for validation via approval, acceptance, and perfectionism cause me to be stagnant in personal and spiritual growth. In many instances, I traded God's directions and words for others. The calling on YOUR life is just that YOURS. You don't need anyone else's permission to be what God has already ordained. Everyone that God to wear a mantle in kingdom was not perfect, but it was the imperfections and their willingness to trust that made them the perfect fit for the position. Be okay with doing what's best for you, and if it's a no, that's all you need. You don't have to explain why it's a no. Watch how peaceful and uncomplicated life becomes, because choosing you filters out the takers in your life and reduces heartache.

"For am I now seeking the approval of man, or of God? Or am I trying to please man? If I were still trying to please man, I would not be a servant of Christ." **-Galatians 1:10**

Today's Reflection

M T W Th F S Su   Date: _____

How has pleasing people affected your growth?

_____

_____

_____

_____

_____

_____

_____

_____

_____

_____

_____

_____

_____

_____

_____

_____

_____

_____

_____

_____

_____

_____

_____

DAY 25

When I look back on a consistent struggle that has plagued my life it was so clear yet very hard to accept. My struggle was just plain going against myself, I was the problem that created the habits that fueled the chaos. No matter if it was something someone was asking me to do, something I needed to do, or just basic interactions... I found myself feeling like no but saying yes. In some instances, I wanted to say no, but said I would think about it. I spent so much of my life overextending myself to show others that I was a good person. When the truth is many of the people that I was jumping through hoops for were takers. Takers are the type of people who only recognize when you say no. I used to give them everything, even what I really didn't "have" to give, and the first time I said no, they called me selfish.

My lack of boundaries has kept me in places and relationships that felt uncomfortable, unsafe, uninhabitable, and showed no room for growth or elevation. God would grant me discernment about people, I would know I need to separate myself. Yet, if they called, I answered. In my mind, I needed to have a reason to say no that they would understand. Otherwise, they would believe I was acting funny. I learned these lessons the hard way and now understand that not to be true.

You don't have to explain to others why you are doing what you do. All you have to do is trust God and trust yourself. We become double-minded when we try to please others outside of God. Don't overextend yourself. Say no, and don't explain the no. No is a complete sentence! Be ok with each version of you. Search deep and ask yourself what need are you meeting for yourself by over extending, saying yes, or going along to get along. For me, it was that sense of being a good person, the need for validation, and the need to feel seen and needed.

It sounds funny, but very often I got the opposite. I felt unseen, unheard, unappreciated, and taken for granted. I would typically take so much until I created an internal mob that I would release to attack and destroy anything and everyone in sight. So much anger, so much hurt, so much shame, so much confusion. Had I just learned the area of boundaries, life would be different, I'm sure. Today, I answer no first, and allow myself to process what is needed from me, what the possible results are, and if this is what God wants me to do. You never want to be heartless, but it's important to learn how to use your heart less. I encourage you today as you shine light on your struggles that keep showing up in your habits. Dig through the habits, the cycles, and locate the root. When did I first experience this? What were the driving factors for the choices made? What have been the results, and what results do you truly desire? For me, I learned that how God sees you is all that matters, people want me on the judge panel casting their vote from the deeds. God knows your heart, and His concern is the work that you did in His Kingdom, not for man.

"For it is by grace you have been saved, through faith—and this is not from yourselves, it is the gift of God— not by works, so that no one can boast." **-Ephesians 2:8-9**

Today's Reflection

M   T   W   Th   F   S   Su   Date: _____

When you look back, what repeated struggle do you continue to have? What habits contribute to that?

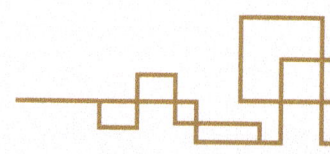

Today's Reflection

M T W Th F S Su

Date: _____

Continued...

_____

_____

_____

_____

_____

_____

_____

_____

_____

_____

_____

_____

_____

_____

_____

_____

_____

_____

_____

_____

_____

_____

DAY 26

My childhood wounds and trauma wreaked havoc on my adult life. It's easier to identify and address the surface-level behaviors and thoughts. Yet what we don't always recognize is that many of the ways we think and act are just the tip of the iceberg. What we don't see is what drives us the most. My childhood trauma and wounds have caused me to lack boundaries, overgive, overstay, and settle for functional dysfunction. I tend to revert back to familiar people, places, and things when being challenged to elevate. I used to be frustrated and just plain disgusted because I felt like I was regressing when I encountered certain situations. What God showed me was that as He grows within me, there are some areas of my life that He needs to know that I can STAND and be ready for the next level.

It can be difficult to move to the next lesson or level when you still haven't mastered the fundamentals from the last one. Don't be hard on yourself, understand there will be times that you have reread a chapter, repeat a season, not because you are regressing but because you need to retain and apply the lesson in order to move on. Continue toward trust that God is with you, and that there is no giant too big to conquer. So get rid of the word impossible... because there is nothing about God and his promises that is impossible. Keep pushing towards God, no matter your shortcomings, worries, or current place. Remember, it's the places we try to hide the most that God wants to use us. When things get too heavy or feel impossible, step aside and let God bear that weight and trust the journey to purpose.

"With God all things are possible." **-Matthew 19:26**

Today's Reflection

M   T   W   Th   F   S   Su   Date: _____

What area in your life seems impossible to fix? Why?

_____

_____

_____

_____

_____

_____

_____

_____

_____

_____

_____

_____

_____

_____

_____

_____

_____

_____

_____

_____

_____

_____

Anxiety is defined as a form of fear that causes dread or uneasiness. Life can be very unpredictable without our help. For years, I worried about the what if's. What if I lose my job? What if something happens to someone I love, What if this man leaves me? What if I don't have enough money? What if they don't like me? What if I Fail? I have lost sleep, hair, weight, money, and time because of anxiety about What IF. When I have discovered that you are only as strong as your source. When your what if's arise who are you calling? Many times I noticed I was calling my sister, my friends, I'm looking on the internet for answers instead of going to the one that could actually calm and resolve any situation... GOD. Anxiety is a human reaction, just remember God is the supernatural antidote. I encourage you to take a "Then God" attitude to help reduce anxiety. What if that job lets you go... Then God. What if that relationship fails? Then God. What if the bills are due? Then God! Rest in knowing that God has the strategy. He is still fighting on your behalf. Nothing catches him by surprise, he has already equipped you with the tools you need for the battle. This is where TRUST activates and your own understanding requires deactivation. There a few things that happen when we operate in anxiousness:

1. You become stuck- You become so stuck on the What if's that you ignore when God gives you directives. the enemy will always delay what it can not destroy
2. You become double minded- You begin to question the provision that God has over you life
3. Lose Faith- You begin to discharge faith and compromise the heart, doubt God, and the purpose.

Sometimes the plot is not to kill you, but to keep you so drained that you never finish. The word expresses to us that God didn't give us the spirit of fear, but of power, love, and sound mind. I encourage you today to put down your human process and trust in God's divine provision and promise over everything concerning you.

"Do not be anxious about anything, but in every situation, by prayer and petition, with thanksgiving, present your requests to God. And the peace of God, which transcends all understanding, will guard your hearts and your minds in Christ Jesus." **-Philippians 4:6-7**

Today's Reflection

M T W Th F S Su   Date: _____

What has caused you anxiety lately?

_____

_____

_____

_____

_____

_____

_____

_____

_____

_____

_____

_____

_____

_____

_____

_____

_____

_____

_____

_____

DAY 28

As I have continued to build the relationship with God and journey on this path called purpose. The area that I feel that I renew and reset my expectations with God consists of how I see myself. God has many elements that all collectively combine to who He is. As I journey with God, I am understanding that the God who showed up for me when I needed deliverance is also the same God who showed up for me when my children needed food or bills needed to be paid. He is also the same God who showed up for me when I was suffering with heartache from my daughter's death, and the same God who protects me from dangers seen and unseen. I'm learning to stop putting limitations on God. I prayed for breakthroughs, literally saying God, if you just do this, I will not ask you for anything else. The breakthrough happened, I celebrated, and then I put God down. I stopped praying as much, I stopped seeking His word, listening for His voice, and being disobedient.

In my earlier experience, I thought God was just a deliverance God. He just makes a way out of no way. As I began to grow in Him, life began "life-ing" on steroids. I began to see God in different ways, He was more than the God who makes a way out of no way. He was a God of peace, of power, of hope, of direction, of sustainment, of protection, of clarity, of discernment, and so much more. Just like He was fully capable of pulling me out of a situation, He is also capable of sustaining me through it. I was so focused on what I couldn't do, which at times turned into me feeling defeated or unbelieving of God's word. When the truth is it's not all on me, Philippians 4:13 says, "I can do all things through Christ who strengthens me." This means we must learn to lean into God. Nowhere does that scripture say, I can do this on my own." We encounter seasons where we feel exposed and uncovered, but God is with us. Learn to surrender it all to Him, and expect that He will show up exactly how He sees fit. If you doubt the magnitude of God, then you will doubt who He is calling you to be. God has layers, and so do you. Your purpose is greater than your flaws, what you've been through, and what you're used to. How can you have faith and expectation of who God is and what God will do if you don't believe and recognize who you are? By giving yourself permission to be the YOU that God called you to be, you also surrender to God's will with pure expectations that His provision is the promise.

"Have I not commanded you? Be strong and courageous. Do not be afraid; do not be discouraged, for the Lord your God will be with you wherever you go."
-Joshua 1:6

Today's Reflection

M T W Th F S Su   Date: _____

What areas do you need to renew your faith and expectations of God?

_____

_____

_____

_____

_____

_____

_____

_____

_____

_____

_____

_____

_____

_____

_____

_____

_____

_____

_____

_____

_____

_____

_____

DAY 29

Childhood traumas can significantly affect how we navigate adulthood. It affects how we regulate emotions that manifest in anxiety, mood swings, or poor stress management. Childhood trauma can lead to challenges in forming and maintaining healthy relationships. This sometimes looks like trust issues, fear of abandonment, or patterns of emotional dependency or avoidance. Mental disorders- There is a strong correlation between childhood trauma and the development of mental health disorders in adulthood, such as depression, anxiety, PTSD, and borderline personality disorder. Poor Self-Image and Identity: Traumatic experiences can negatively impact self-esteem and self-worth. Very often feeling of inadequacy, shame, or having a distorted self-image. Poor Coping Mechanisms and behavioral patterns. Unaddressed childhood traumas lead to substance abuse, compulsive behaviors, or self-harm, choosing toxic relationships, or engaging in self-sabotaging behaviors. Not to mention the numerous physical health issues.

For me, it showed up in toxic relationships, overdeveloped strengths, anda lack of boundaries. I stayed in places too long, I took too much, and I never asked for help, and often took on others' responsibilities as my own. This keeps you in a constant state of fatigue, and when you are tired, it's hard to hear from God. Even harder to reap what you have sown where there is no rest. I encourage you today to sit with yourself and unpack all the things that you try to hide, not because you just need to get over it, but because they are keeping you chained to hurt when God has promised you peace, love, joy, abundance, and so much more. Everything NEW!

"Therefore, if anyone is in Christ, he is a new creation; old things have passed away; behold, all things have become new." **-2 Corinthians 5:17**

Today's Reflection

M T W Th F S Su

Date: _____

What's a trauma you experienced in childhood?
How does that affect you now?

_____

_____

_____

_____

_____

_____

_____

_____

_____

_____

_____

_____

_____

_____

_____

_____

_____

_____

_____

_____

DAY 30

In the depths of self-discovery's embrace, A journey embarked, to find my own trace. In pursuit of oneself, I wander and roam, Seeking the essence of who destined to become. Like a river that flows through the heart of time, I navigate the currents, seeking the sublime. Unraveling layers, shedding masks I've worn, Unveiling the rawness, the truth that's been sworn. In the depth of thoughts, I wander and explore, unpacking the mysteries, seeking something more. Through the valleys of doubts, and the peaks of elation, I find fragments of self, in every revelation. Amidst the chaos and noise of the world's demands, I search for the whispers of my soul's command. In solitude's embrace, I find solace and peace, A sanctuary where my true self finds release. In the mirror's reflection, I see glimpses of light, The shadows of the past, fading into the night. Embracing imperfections, embracing my flaws, I find strength in vulnerability's applause. For in pursuit of oneself, there lies the key, To unlock the treasures of authenticity. Embracing passions, dreams, and desires, I weave a tapestry of self that never tires. And as I journey on, through life's winding road, I embrace the lessons, the stories yet untold. In pursuit of oneself, I'll forever roam, Discovering the depths of who I've always known. Forever in the pursuit of ME - in alignment with God's divine decree.....................Who are you?

Today's Reflection

M T W Th F S Su   Date: _____

Who are you? Who do you want to become?

_____

_____

_____

_____

_____

_____

_____

_____

_____

_____

_____

_____

_____

_____

_____

_____

_____

_____

_____

_____

_____

_____

Beautiful Chaos

In the realm of swirling shades and vibrant tones,
Where harmony and disorder intertwine,
Lies a canvas of chaos, where beauty is sown,
A tapestry of inconsistencies, both wild and divine.
Chaotic actions,
Creating a masterpiece that defies control,
A symphony of emotions, a vibrant rush,
Where order and randomness beautifully enroll.

In the chaos, there's a rhythm that beckons,
A melody that whispers to our souls,
It's in the unexpected, the uncharted seconds,
That beauty emerges, as chaos unfolds.
Like a kaleidoscope, spinning in delight,
The fragments of me align and collide,
Creating a spectacle, a breathtaking sight,
Where beauty and chaos forever reside.
So let us embrace the beautiful chaos,
With open hearts and minds, unafraid, For within its depths,
a world of wonder grows,
Where harmony and disorder are artfully portrayed.

In the chaos, we find the essence of life,
A reminder that imperfection is our muse,
For it is through chaos that we truly thrive,
And discover beauty in the unpredictable hues.
So let us revel in this beautiful mess,
Embrace the chaos with arms open wide,
For it is in the chaos that you find yourself,
A symphony of beauty, forever amplified.

Notes

Notes

Notes

_____
_____
_____
_____
_____
_____
_____
_____
_____
_____
_____
_____
_____
_____
_____
_____
_____
_____
_____
_____
_____
_____

Notes

Notes

Notes

Notes

Notes

www.ingramcontent.com/pod-product-compliance
Lightning Source LLC
Chambersburg PA
CBHW041122120626
46547CB00019B/2818